Text: *Keith Fergus*
Series editor: *Tony Bowerman*
Photographs: *Keith Fergus/*
www.scottishhorizons.photoshelter.com
Paul Saunders Photography/
www.paulsaundersphotography.com,
iStock/Getty Images, Shutterstock, Dreamstime,
Wikipedia Commons

Design: *Carl Rogers*

© Northern Eye Books Limited 2016

Keith Fergus has asserted his rights under the Copyright, Designs and Patents Act, 1988 to be identified as the author of this work. All rights reserved.

This book contains mapping data licensed from the Ordnance Survey with the permission of the Controller of Her Majesty's Stationery Office. © Crown copyright 2016. All rights reserved. Licence number 100047867

Northern Eye Books
ISBN 978-1-908632-42-5

A CIP catalogue record for this book is available from the British Library.

Cover: *Loch Lomond at dusk seen from Millarochy (Walk 4)*

Important Advice: The routes described in this book are undertaken at the reader's own risk. Walkers should take into account their level of fitness, wear suitable footwear and clothing, and carry food and water. It is also advisable to take the relevant OS map with you in case you get lost and leave the area covered by our maps.

Whilst every care has been taken to ensure the accuracy of the route directions, the publishers cannot accept responsibility for errors or omissions, or for changes in the details given. Nor can the publisher and copyright owners accept responsibility for any consequences arising from the use of this book.

If you find any inaccuracies in either the text or maps, please write or email us at the address below. Thank you.

This edition published in 2016 by
Northern Eye Books Limited
Northern Eye Books, Tattenhall, Cheshire CH3 9PX
Email: tony@northerneyebooks.com

For sales enquiries, please call 01928 723 744

www.northerneyebooks.co.uk
www.top10walks.co.uk

 Twitter: @outdoorfergie
@Northerneyeboo
@Top10walks

Contents

Scotland's First National Park 4
Top 10 Walks: Lochside Walks 6
1. **Luss** 8
2. **Balloch Castle Country Park** ... 14
3. **Loch Lomond NNR** 20
4. **Balmaha** & **Milarrochy** 26
5. **Sallochy Wood** & **Dun Maoil** .. 32
6. **Along Loch Katrine** 38
7. **Loch Ard** 44
8. **Loch Katrine** & **Loch Arklet** 50
9. **Inversnaid** & **Loch Lomond** 54
10. **Loch Venachar** 58
Useful Information 64

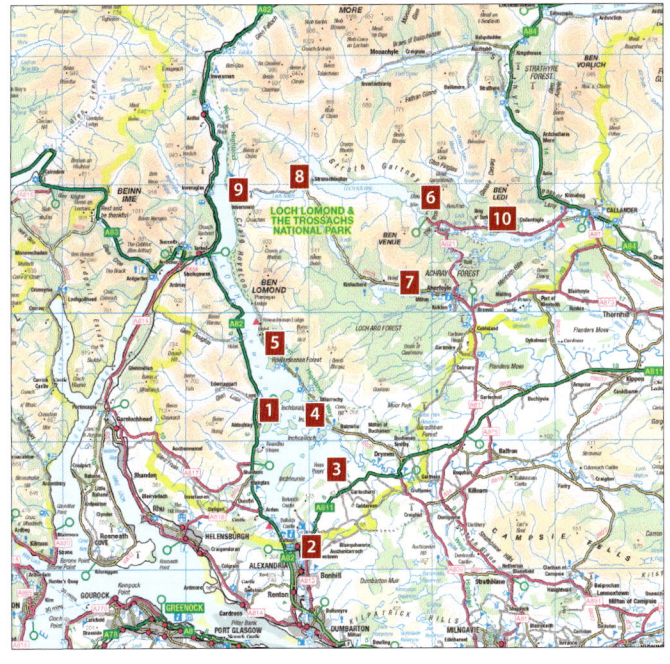

4 ♦ TOP 10 WALKS **LOCHSIDE WALKS**

Scotland's first National Park

IN 2002 LOCH LOMOND AND THE TROSSACHS became Scotland's first National Park (the Cairngorms became Scotland's second, and so far only other National Park, a year later).

It covers an area of 720 square miles and boasts 40 mountains over 2,500 feet in height including some of Scotland's most iconic Munro's and Corbett's: Ben Lomond, the craggy peaks of Ben Vorlich and Stuc a Chroin above Loch Earn, big, brutish and beautiful mountains like Ben Lui, Stob Binnien and Cruach Ardrain and the incomparable Ben Arthur (better known as The Cobbler), to name but a few.

Also within the National Park's confines are around 50 rivers and burns, 3 National Nature Reserves, 2 Forest Parks and 22 large lochs (plus numerous smaller lochs and lochans), including Loch Lomond, Loch Katrine and Loch Venachar, all of which hosts to a huge array of wildlife.

This breathtaking scenery and wildlife attracts around 4 million visitors each year.

Loch Lomond and the Arrochar Alps

Lochs and Lochans

The distinctive characteristics of Loch Lomond and The Trossachs National Park's landscape have been formed over several hundred million years.

The area contains freshwater and sea lochs (the National Park boasts 39 miles of coastline), including Loch Lomond — at 28 miles long and 5 miles wide, the largest body of freshwater in the UK. Add to this Loch Arklet, Loch Ard, Loch Katrine and Loch Venachar and you have an array of beautiful water with breathtaking scenery, wonderful wildlife and some of Scotland's finest walks.

> *"What would the world be, once bereft*
> *Of wet and of wildness? Let them be left,*
> *O let them be left, wildness and wet;*
> *Long live the weeds and the wilderness yet."*
>
> Gerard Manley Hopkins, *Inversnaid*, 1881

TOP 10 Walks: Lochs and Lochans

There are twenty-two lochs within the Loch Lomond and The Trossachs National Park. However, several of these are surrounded by a rough, rugged terrain making them less than ideal for a satisfying walk.

Instead, the ten walks chosen here cover five key lochs, all of which provide fantastic routes in and around their shores. All the walks have their own distinctive attributes, highlighting the area's natural beauty, flora, fauna and fascinating history. Don't miss them.

Luss — page 8

Balloch Castle Country Park — page 14

Loch Lomond NNR — page 20

Balmaha & Milarrochy — page 26

Sallochy Wood & Dun Maoil — page 32

Along Loch Katrine — page 38

Loch Ard — page 44

Loch Katrine & Loch Arklet — page 50

Inversnaid & Loch Lomond — page 54

Loch Venachar — page 58

Luss beach grants a superb view of Loch Lomond and Ben Lomond

walk 1

Luss

A straightforward but picturesque walk around one of Loch Lomondside's prettiest and most popular villages

What to expect:
Clear lochside and woodland paths throughout, plus one short section of beach

Distance/time: 4.5 kilometres/2¾ miles. Allow 1¼ hours

Start: The large pay and display car park in Luss, which can get very busy, particularly during the summer months. Alternative parking is limited within the village

Grid ref: NS 359 931

Ordnance Survey Map: Explorer OL 38 Loch Lomond *South Dumbarton & Helensburgh Drymen & Cove*

After the walk: Pub and hotel in Luss

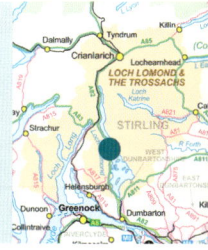

Walk outline
This fascinating and easy walk circumnavigates the attractive village of Luss following good paths through a diverse array of landscape. Beginning on Loch Lomondside the route crosses a section of beach before visiting the secluded wooded glen of The Glebe. From here a lovely section of the Luss Water continues to the Quarry Path, which leads through more fine woodland back into Luss. The scenery is magnificent throughout.

Luss
Although many will recognise Luss as the setting for the 1980-90s Scottish Television drama *Take the High Road*, a settlement here can be traced back to medieval times. Luss was originally known as Clachan Dhu (The Dark Village) as it sat in the shadow of the surrounding hills. The present village dates from the 18th and 19th centuries when houses were built by local landowners, the Colquhouns, for the slate quarry and mill workers and their families. Many of these attractive cottages remain and Luss is now a Conservation Village. It is a fantastic place for a wander.

Luss pier

Mute swans

The Walk

1. Walk past **Luss Visitor Centre** to the car park's northeastern extremity and onto a lovely little **beach beside Loch Lomond**. Here there is a dazzling view across the loch to Ben Lomond and Conic Hill. Turn right, walk along the sand to its end at **Luss Pier**.

2. Go straight across a road then follow a paved track alongside Loch Lomond, passing several attractive cottages. It then veers right past **Clan Colquhoun Heritage and Visitor Centre**.

The museum is located in a 17th century cottage, thought to be the oldest in Luss. It details the turbulent history of the clan, from the 12th century to the present day.

Keep on through a gate where the track culminates at a narrow road beside the attractive **Luss Parish Church**.

It is thought that there has been a holy structure here since 510AD, having been founded by St Kessog. The church we see today was built in 1875 by Sir James Colquhoun of Luss, and is dedicated to Colquhoun's father (also James) who drowned in 1873 after a hunting expedition on Loch Lomond. It is worth stepping inside the church as the complex roof is fashioned from Scots Pine to resemble an upturned boat while there are also a number of charming stained glass windows. An exploration of the kirkyard is also recommended, where lies an 11th century Viking hogback grave while the earliest stones date from the 7th and 8th century.

© Crown copyright and/or database right 2016. All rights reserved. Licence number 100047867

Composition in blue: *Loch Lomond from Luss beach*

3. Bear left on to a road (signposted for the River Path), which swings right to run alongside the gorgeous, wooded **Luss Water**. After 50 metres turn left to cross a **wooden footbridge** over the river into a beautiful open area of grassland surrounded by woodland, with lots of wildflowers and insects and a good place for a picnic.

This lovely, tranquil spot is known as The Glebe. Between 1993 and 2006 the area was inaccessible after the bridge had been washed away. Within that time the land returned to its natural state and today, with the bridge reinstated, The Glebe consists of loch shore, riverbank, oak woodland and meadow.

Follow a gravel path to a **large cross** and here it splits.

4. Take either path and walk around **The Glebe**, enjoying an abundance of wildflowers, birdlife, some wonderful scenery plus some intriguing poems and **sculptures**.

Back at the cross, exit The Glebe across the bridge and turn left.

Pier group?: *Luss is a bustling spot on a lovely warm summer's day*

Go through a gate from where a firm **riverside path** continues south away from Luss through lovely woodland, with wildflowers lining the path and fine views of Cruach Dubh.

The path soon veers right and then climbs a flight of stone steps to reach the main **Luss Road**.

5. Carefully cross here, turn left then right through a gate onto the **Quarry Path**. This fantastic wooded path heads alongside the south bank of the **Luss Water** soon crossing a **footbridge** over a tributary burn. Continue through an underpass beneath the **A82** after which the path climbs above the Luss Water.

In due course it is crossed via a bridge near an impressive **gorge and waterfall** and then passes the site of an old quarry, with large mounds of slate still evident.

After climbing a steep flight of **steps** continue through marvellous woodland all the way to a gate.

6. Once through cross a minor road then bear right onto another path, which runs parallel to the road.

Walk 1 – **Luss** ♦ 13

The path heads down through another gate and then crosses a **footbridge** over the A82. Drop steeply down steps to an access road beside **Luss Primary School**. Turn right, walk to the main **Luss Road**, turn left and return to the car park to complete the walk. ♦

Sacred isle?

It's thought that the Irish missionary Saint Kessog arrived on the shores of Loch Lomond around 1,500 years ago bringing Christianity to the area. He settled on the nearby island of Inchtavannach and was buried there after his death. His body was embalmed in sweet herbs, which supposedly grew and covered his grave, bestowing the settlement with the name Luss, from the Gaelic 'lus', meaning herb.

14 ♦ TOP 10 WALKS

Misty dawn over Loch Lomond and Balloch Castle Country Park

walk 2

Balloch Castle Country Park

Balloch Castle Country Park forms the focal point of a simple, beautiful walk beside Loch Lomond

What to expect:
Well-maintained, mainly level riverbank, lochside and woodland paths, line the route

Distance/time: 7.5 kilometres/4¾ miles. Allow 2 hours

Start: Large free car park at 'Loch Lomond Shores', Balloch

Grid ref: NS 383 822

Ordnance Survey Map: Explorer OL 38 Loch Lomond South *Dumbarton & Helensburgh Drymen & Cove*

After the walk: Pubs and hotel in Balloch

Walk outline

One of the most appealing low-level walks within the National Park leaves from Loch Lomond Shores (which grants one of the finest views along Loch Lomond) and travels around the wide-open spaces of Balloch Castle Country Park. Superb paths line the route allowing the walker to disengage the brain and enjoy the crisp, clean air, beautiful woodland, exceptional wildlife (including roe deer and red squirrels) and some truly breathtaking views.

Balloch Castle Country Park

Comprising 200 acres of semi-natural and ornamental woodland and open parkland, Balloch Castle Country Park was laid out as a private estate in the early 19th century by John Buchanan, a wealthy Glasgow businessman, who also built Balloch Castle. It was designated a Country Park in 1980. This beautifully designed landscape has changed little since and grants fantastic views across Loch Lomond. Pipistrelle and brown long-eared bats hunt the grounds. Seventy-three species of bird have also been recorded in and around the park including chiffchaff, willow warbler, wood warbler, blackcap and nuthatch.

Venison burgers

Nuthatch

The Walk

1. From the car park at **Loch Lomond Shores Gateway Centre** take the **lochside walkway**, passing several shops and the modern **Drumkinnon Tower**. *Here take time to relish the sumptuous view along Loch Lomond to Ben Lomond, Scotland's southernmost Munro.*

Beyond the tower follow the **cycle/walkway** (also part of the **John Muir Way**) alongside the loch. When it splits keep right and continue along **Ben Lomond Way**.

2. Cross this road and follow a parkland road towards the **River Leven**. As the road sweeps right, ignore a path to the left but after another 30 metres take the next lefthand path. Follow this through woodland alongside the languid flow of the river.

The River Leven (from the Gaelic Leamha, meaning 'elm bank') runs for approximately six miles between Loch Lomond and the River Clyde. It was exploited by the huge textile industry that existed along the Vale of Leven during the Industrial Revolution — in its heyday it employed over 7000 people and in one year 165 million yards of cloth and 20 million pounds of cotton were dyed and printed. Today it is regarded as one of the Central Belt's premier sea trout and salmon rivers.

0 ———————————————— 1km
———————————————— ½ mile

© Crown copyright and/or database right 2016. All rights reserved. Licence number 100047867

Walk 2 – **Balloch Castle Country Park** ♦ 17

Chattering stream: *Waterfalls cascade down the Balloch Burn towards Loch Lomond*

Keep alongside the river until the path reaches a picnic area. Here turn left through a car park then, just before **Balloch Bridge**, go right to reach **Balloch Road** at **Balloch village centre**.

3. Turn left, take the bridge across the river (where there is a great view of the Luss Hills) then immediately turn left into **Balloch Castle Country Park** (signposted Balloch House).

Take a path along the river's east bank where you may see swans and migrating geese. After 200 metres cross a road into woodland and head north. *Oak, ash, elm and sycamore dominate the woodland with scatterings of beech and Scots pine.*

At a junction bear left after which the river is soon left behind and the path continues alongside **Loch Lomond** with superb views across the park to Balloch Castle.

4. Just before an **old slipway** and **boathouse** (now a café) keep straight on (leaving the John Muir Way, which

Northern lights: *The Aurora Borealis colours the 1950s' steamship 'Maid of the Loch'*

peels to the right) through a mixture of parkland and woodland.

After another 300 metres take a track on the left (marked with a red arrow) and follow this to the **Balloch Burn**. Here a path swings right and climbs gradually to the right of the burn. *During spring the burn is bounded by ramsons (wild garlic) and their pungent aroma fills the air.*

In due course the path swings sharp right then left to run beside a **tributary of the Balloch Burn**. The tributary is soon crossed via **stepping-stones** from where a path climbs to a junction, marked with a blue arrow.

5. Keep right onto a path and when this splits go right and follow a track to a car park.

Beyond stands **Balloch Castle and Gardens**, *which are very much worth exploration. The original castle was built nearby in 1238 and was the historic home of the Earls of Lennox. It was sold to John Colquhoun of Luss in 1652, subsequently falling into disrepair. In the early 19th century John Buchanan of Ardoch purchased the estate and used stone from the walls of the ruined castle to build a mansion, now known as Balloch Castle. At*

Walk 2 – **Balloch Castle Country Park** ♦ 19

the time of writing it is closed to the public but the adjacent gardens are wonderful, as is the expansive view across Loch Lomond.

6. To continue the walk turn left from the car park, follow the main park access road through a wonderful **avenue of trees** for 1km, exiting right onto **Drymen Road**. Follow this through **Balloch**, re-crossing **Balloch Bridge** then retrace your steps back to the start to complete the walk. ♦

From loch to sea

Balloch translates from the Gaelic bealach *as 'the pass' and it's thought that the River Leven, which flows from Loch Lomond to the River Clyde at Dumbarton, provided a means for boats to travel from loch to sea. Balloch developed around tourism during the 1800s, primarily through the arrival of the railway and Loch Lomond's steam cruisers. It's still popular with visitors today.*

Net Bay is an ideal spot for a break with views over the loch to to Ben Lomond

walk 3

Loch Lomond NNR

Fascinating history, superb scenery and exceptional wildlife encompass Loch Lomond National Nature Reserve

What to expect:
Field paths (where livestock may graze) and tracks, some of which can be muddy plus minor road

Distance/time: 7.25 kilometres/4½ miles. Allow 2 hours

Start: The Kilmaronock Millennium Hall Car Park. Parking is free. Alternative parking is limited within the village

Grid ref: NS 429 862

Ordnance Survey Map: Explorer OL 38 Loch Lomond South *Dumbarton & Helensburgh Drymen & Cove*

After the walk: Coffee shop in Gartocharn, pubs/hotels in Drymen and Balloch

Walk outline

The little village of Gartocharn, sitting at the southern edge of the National Park, bestows a fine start point to this lovely route. The scenic (if at times boggy) Aber Path leads to the small settlement of Aber then into Loch Lomond National Nature Reserve. Here an excellent woodland path heads along the banks of Loch Lomond to Net Bay. Quiet roads (with further exceptional scenery) return to Gartocharn.

Loch Lomond National Nature Reserve

Taking in rich habitats such as loch, river bank, floodplain, woodland and grassland the Loch Lomond National Nature Reserve is a wildlife-watcher's dream. The floodplain of the Endrick Water flows into Loch Lomond and is home to sedge-warbler, reed bunting, waterfowl (including migrating Greenland white-fronted, greylag and pink-footed geese), osprey and sporadic sightings of otters. Shore Wood, as well as the reserve's five wooded islands (including Inchcailloch and Aber Isle), contain stands of oak and birch where warblers, redstarts and spotted flycatcher thrive. Small pearl-bordered fritillary butterflies also breed on the reserve.

Aber path

Small pearl bordered fritillary

The Walk

1. From the **Kilmaronock Millennium Hall Car Park**, which sits off Church Road in Gartocharn village centre, exit right onto Church Road then turn left, just after the **Millennium Hall**, onto the 'Aber Right of Way Nature Reserve' track. *Here there is a stunning view of Ben Lomond.*

Shortly afterwards the track swings left and so keep straight on through a gate from where the right of way path descends gently northwest along a field and through gorgeous open countryside (livestock may be grazing, so keep dogs on leads).

It then continues through woodland *(home to common spotted orchid during spring and summer)*. Beyond a gate a path now runs along the left edge of another field. At its end, go through a gate and cross the **Aber Dam Bridge** over the **Aber Burn**.

The Aber Burn was dammed to provide water to power a local grain mill. It was also the point where, in 1685, the Earl of Argyll and his army decided against attacking the Government troops of James VII of Scotland. A nationwide conflict had arisen after many deemed the King's Catholic regime would undermine the Protestant faith in Scotland.

2. After another gate turn right onto a minor road, at the small settlement of **Aber**.

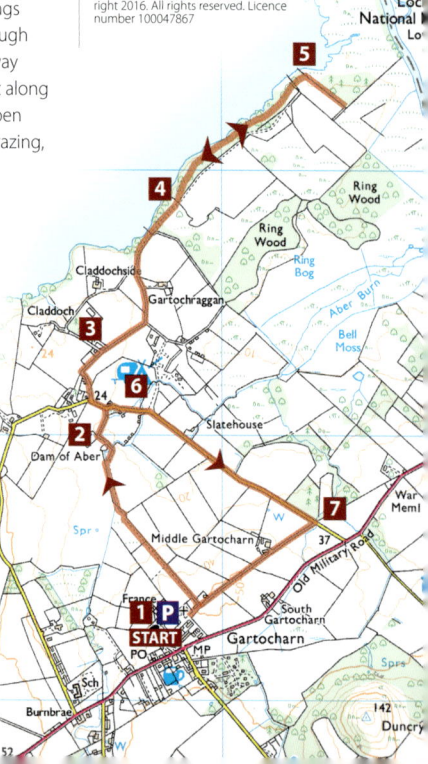

© Crown copyright and/or database right 2016. All rights reserved. Licence number 100047867

Walk 3 – **Loch Lomond NNR** ♦ 23

In a green shade: *Dappled sunlight falls across the path in Shore Wood*

Aber is a Brittonic word that means 'a river meeting a larger body of water', in this case referring to the Endrick Water flowing into Loch Lomond.

At the next junction, beside a cottage, keep left and when the road splits go right into **Loch Lomond National Nature Reserve**. A quiet road passes several houses through a mixture of woodland and open countryside.

3. When the road forks take the right branch and continue for another 300 metres, at which point the road narrows to a rough track and drops down through a gate.

4. After a further 50 metres take the wooden gate to the left of a metal gate into the beautiful surrounds of **Shore Wood**. Walk northeast along the shores of **Loch Lomond**, through stunning oak woodland, home to wood sorrel and harebell.

When the water level is low the stonework of an old jetty is visible. Here, during the 1800s, barges were loaded with locally quarried sandstone that was shipped to

Sublime span: *From Gartocharn the panorama includes Loch Lomond, the Luss Hills, 'The Cobbler' and Ben Lomond*

Balloch and then on to Glasgow, where the stone was used to construct many of the city's buildings.

5. After 1 kilometre the path splits. To the left is **Net Bay**, a bench and an exceptional view of Conic Hill, Ben Lomond and the Endrick Water, the largest river to flow into Loch Lomond. Here you may spot wildfowl and cattle grazing at the river and loch edge.

Head back to the main track. For a **short detour** go left then right through a gate and follow a field path (which can be muddy) for 300 metres to the **Endrick Viewpoint**, a fine spot to view the surrounding countryside and one of Scotland's best plant-rich wet meadows.

Return to the **main path**, go left and retrace your steps for 1.5 kilometres back to **Aber** at NS 425 871.

6. Keep straight on here, along this minor road, passing an **old mill** (now a striking house) and the entrance of a caravan site. The road, flanked by hedgerows, climbs gradually towards the A811 through scenic countryside — *keep an eye out here for buzzards.*

Walk 3 – **Loch Lomond NNR** ♦ 25

7. Approximately 150 metres before the **A811** turn right onto a track, which rises gradually back towards Gartocharn. *The height gained bestows perhaps the finest view of the walk with The Luss Hills, Ben Lomond and The Cobbler forming an impressive barrier to the north. It is also a good place to watch migrating geese.*

The track ends at **Church Road** beside the **Millennium Hall Car Park**, to complete the walk. ♦

Lovely village

The idyllic village of Gartocharn is surrounded by beautiful countryside and is a lovely spot to wile away a few hours. Its name translates from Gaelic as 'the place of the humped hill' and it used to be home to a corn mill. Gartocharn's roots also lie in sandstone quarrying and agriculture — many of the field enclosures here have changed very little in more than 140 years.

Craigie Forts presents a breathtaking view of Loch Lomond

walk 4

Balmaha & Milarrochy

Balmaha village and Milarrochy Bay bookend this gorgeous walk, which includes the viewpoint of Craigie Fort

What to expect: Excellent lochside and woodland paths, one steep ascent/descent plus a short section of minor road

Distance/time: 5.5 kilometres/3½ miles. Allow 1½ hours

Start: Large car park in the centre of Balmaha. Parking is free but it can get busy, particularly in summer. Alternative parking is limited within the village

Grid ref: NS 522 009

Ordnance Survey Map: Explorer OL 38 Loch Lomond South *Dumbarton & Helensburgh Drymen & Cove*

After the walk: Pub/hotel in Balmaha

Walk outline

Pleasant woodland and lochside paths lead through the attractive village of Balmaha, which sits on Loch Lomond's eastern shore. After a short section of minor road a steep climb reaches Craigie Fort, and an exceptional panorama across Loch Lomond, before descending back to the loch. Now the West Highland Way extends to Milarrochy Bay's sandy beach, a fine spot for a break before heading back to Balmaha.

Balmaha

There is much conjecture regarding the derivation of the name Balmaha, but is thought to stem from the Gaelic Bealach Mo Cha, meaning 'the pass of Mo Cha', referring to Saint Kentigerna, the daughter of an Irish Prince. Saint Kentigerna emigrated from Ireland during the 8th century and settled on the island of Inchcailloch, which sits just off the shore at Balmaha.

The path network between Balmaha and Milarrochy Bay is superb, and the adjacent woodland is home to oak, alder, goat's willow and an exceptional array of flora and fauna.

Balmaha boat hire

Roe deer fawn

The Walk

1. From the large car park at **Balmaha** walk to its northeastern end where there is a large 'Balmaha' sign and information board. Beyond both turn left onto a path and walk west along the northern edge of the village, through predominantly oak woodland — *during May/early June the carpet of bluebells is spectacular.*

Soon the path zigzags downhill to reach the **B837** at **Balmaha Bay**.

2. Carefully cross the road, go through a gap in a wall and turn right onto the **West Highland Way** beside a viewing platform. *Here you can look out on to the large wooded island of Inchcailloch and watch birdlife such as coot, moorhen and mallard on the loch.*

Inchcailloch translates from Gaelic as 'Island of the Old Woman' and is thought to have been named after St Kentigerna, who established a Christian community on the island during the 8th century. An on demand ferry service runs from Balmaha to Inchailloch and when on the island the remains of a burial ground and a 13th century church (plus an exceptional diversity of flora and fauna) can be seen.

Follow the path to its end as it heads west, away from Balmaha, inbetween the B837 and Loch Lomond.

Now turn left onto a minor road, walk past a cottage and after 100 metres turn right at a waymark.

3. From here the West Highland Way

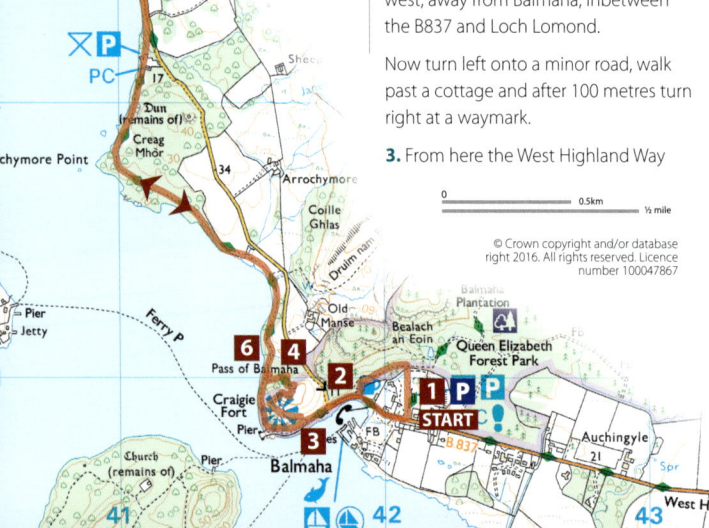

© Crown copyright and/or database right 2016. All rights reserved. Licence number 100047867

Walk 4 – **Balmaha** & **Milarrochy** ♦ 29

Bright blue day: *The jetty and hills at Balmaha*

climbs steeply away from the loch. It rises through more gorgeous woodland, quickly gaining the **summit of Craigie Fort**.

There is scant information regarding the history of Craigie Fort although there seems to be evidence of vitrified remains across the summit, which sits just above the treeline. Here there is a stunning vista, one that extends across Loch Lomond and its many islands to Ben Lomond, the Luss Hills and the Arrochar Alps.

4. Keep on past the summit after which the path bears left and descends north through woodland, soon winding downhill back towards **Loch Lomond**.

Just before reaching the **loch shore** the path splits so keep right to a junction and here go right again.

The West Highland Way continues lochside, north then northwest towards **Milarrochy Bay** through lovely scenery and beside a number of small, sandy beaches, ideal places for a break. There are a few **burns** to cross en route, all of which pose no problems.

Mountain mirror: *Sunset tints the still waters of Loch Lomond at Milarrochy Bay*

In a while the path rounds **Arrochymore Point** and then, after another kilometre, reaches **Milarrochy Bay**, with its long sandy beach. Here there is a **car park**, **boat hire**, **public toilets** and some great views. It is a good spot for a rest.

The oak woodland cloaking the east shore of Loch Lomond near Milarrochy Bay is beautiful to walk through and explore, with scatterings of buttercup, primrose, wood sorrel and bluebell during late spring/early summer, while autumn brings a kaleidoscope of colour. Redstarts, wood warblers, woodpeckers and treecreepers are just some of birdlife that may be spotted.

5. Retrace steps for 2¼ kilometres to the junction of paths at the northern side of Craigie Fort.

6. Here keep straight on along the lochside path, leaving the West Highland Way behind. The route soon crosses a **metal footbridge**, taking you over the loch beside a steep cliff face, with a short, rockier section of path culminating beside the minor road at the western edge of Balmaha.

Walk 4 – **Balmaha** & **Milarrochy** ♦ 31

Turn left and follow this quiet road back towards **Balmaha village centre**, picking up the **West Highland Way** as progress is made.

At the **B837** bear right and walk along the paved path past Balmaha Bay and a fine **bronze statue** of esteemed hillwalker and broadcaster Tom Weir. At a pub/restaurant and village shop carefully cross the B837 back to the start, to complete the walk. ♦

Local hero

Tom Weir MBE was a familiar face to many, primarily because of his long-running Scottish television series 'Weir's Way'. The much-loved climber, author and broadcaster died in 2006 aged 91 having lived for many years in Gartocharn, on the edge of the National Park. After his death a campaign began to build a commemorative statue. More than £70,000 was raised through public appeal and the statue was unveiled in 2014.

A magnificent view along Loch Lomond from the top of Dun Maoil

walk 5

Sallochy Wood & Dun Maoil

A diverse route that takes in lochside, woodland and a superb, little visited viewpoint

What to expect:
Clear paths throughout with a prolonged, yet gradual rise to Dun Maoil

Distance/time: 5.5 kilometres/3½ miles. Allow 1½ hours

Start: Pay and display car park at Sallochy. There is a campsite here, meaning it can get busy, particularly during the summer months

Grid ref: NS 380 958

Ordnance Survey Map: Explorer OL 39 Loch Lomond North *Tyndrum, Crianlarich & Arrochar*

After the walk: Pub/hotel in Rowardennan and Balmaha

Walk outline

Beginning from the shores of Loch Lomond at Sallochy, a good path rises through stunning oak woodland and past the abandoned farmsteads of Wester Sallochy. A wide forest track then climbs onto Dun Maoil, a superb vantage point to take in Loch Lomond and the neighbouring scenery. An easy descent leads to a breathtaking section of the West Highland Way that proceeds easily through wildflower rich woodland back to Sallochy.

Sallochy

Today, Sallochy is a Site of Special Scientific Interest and a Special Area of Conservation due to its woodland. Yet, perhaps surprisingly, during the 19th century it was a bustling hive of industry where every spring women and children coppiced trees and stripped off the oak bark. The tannic acid from the bark was used to fix dyes in the great textile factories along the Vale of Leven. Willow would also have cloaked the lochside (Sallochy comes from the Gaelic *seileach* meaning willow) and was used in the production of creels, chairs, horse bridles and even coffins.

Woodland path

Red squirrel and bluebells

The Walk

1. The route starts from **Sallochy Car Park**, which is two miles southwest of Rowardennan, on the eastern shore of Loch Lomond. Follow the access road towards the Balmaha/Rowardennan road but just before reaching this bear right onto a red/blue waymarked path.

Follow this to the road and once across take another **waymarked woodland path**. This runs to the right of a burn and climbs gently east away from Sallochy through **Rowardennan Forest**.

After 200 metres the path splits so keep right (still following blue/red waymarks), now on a slightly steeper ascent through gorgeous oak, birch and larch woodland.

Keep an eye (and ear) out for greater spotted woodpeckers, red squirrels, roe deer, wood warblers and buzzards. The path soon passes the ruins of Wester Sallochy, which date from the 19th century when they formed part of the industrial landscape of Sallochy. It is thought this site comprised five buildings, one of which may have been a farmhouse and another a limekiln. All were the property of the Duke of Montrose.

A beautiful section of the walk continues through woodland to gain a wide **Forestry Commission track**.

2. Turn left from where it begins to ascend gradually north, with the craggy outcrop of Dun Maoil ahead. *There are*

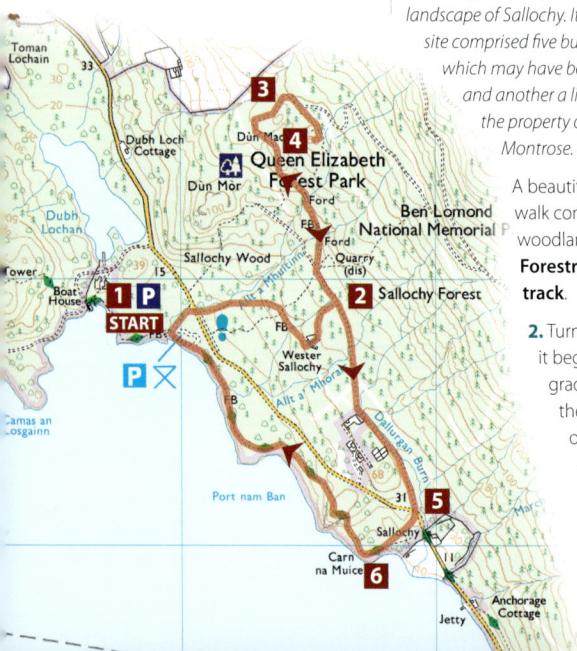

© Crown copyright and/or database right 2016. All rights reserved. Licence number 100047867

Walk 5 – **Sallochy Wood** & **Dun Maoil** ♦ 35

Sunlit glades: *Open, wildflower-rich oak woodland near Sallochy*

glimpses of Loch Lomond through the trees as well as fine views of the Luss Hills.

After 600-metres a blue waymarked path peels away to the left; but instead, stick with the main track as it climb gradually, now following red waymarks. After a further 300-metres the track veers right to reach a waymarked path on the right.

3. Leave the main track from where a short rise through birch trees gains the **summit of Dun Maoil** — there are steep drops on three sides, so take care.

Dun Maoil may translate as 'fort of the brow' or 'the bald fort' and its bare, rocky slopes certainly rise prominently above the treeline of Rowardennan Forest and that of Loch Lomond, which is cloaked in great swathes of woodland. The view is extraordinary, and it is easy to see why it might have been used as a lookout in days gone by. The panorama takes in much of Loch Lomond and its many islands, the big, muscular Arrochar Alps and the familiar profile of Ben Lomond, Scotland's most southerly Munro.

4. Return to the main track, turn left and

Lochside view: *Looking out over Loch Lomond from Sallochy*

retrace your steps along the outward-bound route for a kilometre to the blue/red waymarked path, northeast of **Wester Sallochy**. However do not take the path, instead keep straight on along the track, descending gently southeast.

The track is easily followed through mixed woodland for another kilometre. Once around a **metal barrier** the track culminates at the **Balmaha/ Rowardennan road**.

5. From the right edge of the track, cross the road onto an indistinct path and follow this a short distance down to gain the **West Highland Way**.

6. Turn right here and continue along an excellent path, which heads northwest along a truly delightful section of **Loch Lomond**.

Again oak woodland dominates (many of the trees are over 200 years old), home to redstart, blue and coal tits and where wildflowers, such as bluebell and buttercup, are stunning during May and June. The colours during autumn are also spectacular.

After a short, steep pull (aided by some

Walk 5 – **Sallochy Wood** & **Dun Maoil** ♦ 37

steps) the route continues above Loch Lomond before dropping back down to the shore where it passes several lovely, **stony beaches** with fine views across the loch.

A final, easy wander of 250 metres leads back to the **car park at Sallochy** to complete the walk. ♦

Woodland vision
James Graham, the 3rd Duke of Montrose (1755-1836), planted much of the oak woodland along Loch Lomond's eastern shore (his great grandfather, the 3rd Marquis of Montrose, bought extensive lands around Loch Lomond in 1682). Having been educated at Eton and Trinity College, Graham became MP for Richmond in 1780 then for Great Bedwyn in 1784. He was also Chancellor of Glasgow University between 1781 and 1836.

A summer's day on the banks of Loch Katrine

walk 6

Along **Loch Katrine**

The mountainous landscape surrounding Loch Katrine comes to the fore during this spectacular route

What to expect:
Quiet lochside road and hillside path with one steady ascent/descent

Distance: 10.75 kilometres/6¾ miles. Allow 3 hours

Start: Large pay and display car park at Trossachs Pier, Loch Katrine. It can get very busy, particularly during the summer months

Grid ref: NN 495 072

Ordnance Survey Map: Explorer Explorer OL46 Callander, *Aberfoyle & Lochearnhead, Balquhidder & Strathyre*

After the walk: Restaurant/café at Trossachs Pier

Walk outline

Beginning from Trossachs Pier, which is at the eastern edge of Loch Katrine, a private road travels along the banks of the loch. A steep path then rises onto open hillside above the loch from where easy progress is made with outstanding views towards the Arrochar Alps. Eventually a path drops back down to Loch Katrine from where another scenic section of road leading back to Trossachs Pier.

Loch Katrine and Sir Walter Scott

Loch Katrine lies in the heart of The Trossachs and has been a magnet for visitors ever since Sir Walter Scott published his poem *Lady of the Lake* in 1810. Scott had holidayed in The Trossachs when it was a small, wooded glen that occupied the area in and around Loch Katrine. *Lady of the Lake* centres around the dispute between Roderick Dhu, James Fitz-James and Malcolm Graeme to win the love of Ellen Douglas, and on its publication it became a blockbuster, selling 25,000 copies in the first eight months, with Scott's fame (and that of The Trossachs) growing exponentially.

Paddling in Loch Katrine

Otter on the shore

40 ♦ TOP 10 WALKS **LOCHSIDE** WALKS

The Walk

Trossachs Pier has a shop, cycle hire, café/restaurant and is where the SS Sir Walter Scott sets sail, taking thousands of visitors along Loch Katrine every year — her maiden voyage was in 1900. Loch Katrine is owned by Scottish Water and has been the main reservoir for Glasgow since 1859.

1. Walk through the **car park** keeping to the right of the **ticket office**, then go round a barrier onto the private **water board road**. This is easily followed along the eastern **shore of Loch Katrine**, although keep an eye out for works traffic and cyclists.

The loch is hemmed in by high hills with steep crags to the right, and the road is flanked with birch, oak, rowan and heather. With a superb view of Ben Venue's muscular form, it is easy to see why Sir Walter Scott was so taken with it.

2. In a while the road crosses a **weir** at **Glen Finglas Falls** and shortly afterwards further superb views open out, with several wooded islands, including **Eilean Molach**, dotted along Loch Katrine. Once through a gate beside a deer grid continue, crossing a **bridge** over **Allt Tormaid**.

3. After another 150 metres turn right from the road onto a green waymarked path, which rises steadily up a wooded hillside to gain a junction.

Keep left from where a track continues

© Crown copyright and/or database right. All rights reserved. Licence number 100047867

Walk 6 – **Along Loch Katrine** ♦ 41

On the water: *The 'SS Sir Walter Scott' takes tourists along Loch Katrine*

northwest, above the treeline and **Loch Katrine**, along an easier gradient — *there is a wonderful vista of Ben Venue. Look out for the SS Sir Walter Scott, as well as buzzards, ravens and geese.*

4. Where the track splits in a while, go right and continue on a gentle rise. Keep on under the steep, rocky slopes of **Cro Iolaire** relishing a grandstand view.

Loch Katrine extends towards the Arrochar Alps with The Cobbler, Ben Ime, Beinn Narnain and Ben Vane forming a magnificent backdrop. Ben Lomond, scoured by the deep bowl of Coire Fuar, is also visible — it is simply an exceptional panorama.

5. After 2 kilometres the track ends at its highest point (270-metres). Go around a **wooden barrier** onto a path that descends along a **series of zigzags** — *bestowing a marvellous view of Ben A'an's sharp summit while the vista towards the Arrochar Alps continues.*

Upon reaching a track keep right, go through a gate from where another

Cloud mirror: *A grandstand view along Loch Katrine to the Arrochar Alps*

path drops down through stunning oak and birch woodland. Once across a **burn** the path sweeps left and makes a final gradual descent back to the **Loch Katrine private road**.

6. Turn left (again, watch out for traffic) and follow the road southeast above Loch Katrine, passing the entrance to **Brenachoile Lodge**.

Opposite, on the right side of the road, is a path that drops down to an **old pier** and **boathouse**. *Here a stony beach, with an outstanding view along Loch Katrine, makes for a marvellous place for a break.*

Back on the road keep on for another ¾ kilometre to **Ruinn Dubh Aird**, which is also known as **Brenachoile Point**. Again a path leads down to the loch shore where you can witness The Trossachs landscape that has provided stimulation for numerous artists and writers over the past 200 years.

As well as Sir Walter Scott, others that have taken inspiration from The Trossachs include JMW Turner, Robert Burns, William and Dorothy Wordsworth, Samuel Taylor Coleridge, Charles Dickens, Hans Christian Anderson and Gerard Manley Hopkins. Another visitor was the French writer Jules Verne whose 1877 novel, 'The

Underground City, *is a story about a mining community who lived beneath Loch Katrine.*

7. It is now a couple of miles back to **Trossachs Pier**, where simple navigation allows the fabulous landscape to be enjoyed — with the colours of the adjacent woodland particularly beautiful during autumn — to complete the walk. ♦

Outlaw's refuge?
It is thought that the dense woodland on Eilean Molach (Ellen's Isle) has changed little over the past few centuries. Traditionally, it was a place where fugitives hid. One such fugitive was Ellen Stewart who killed an English soldier while defending her friends and children. Her story was adapted by Sir Walter Scott when he wrote his famous book 'The Lady of the Lake'.

The distinctive outline of Ben Lomond from the shores of Loch Ard

walk 7

Loch Ard

Great paths and tracks make a walk along Loch Ard an absolute joy

What to expect:
Well surfaced, firm paths throughout with a couple of steady ascents

Distance/time: 7kilometres/4¼ miles. Allow 1¾ hours

Start: Forestry Commission Milton car park, Loch Ard Forest

Grid ref: NN 499 010

Ordnance Survey Map: Explorer OL 46 The Trossachs, *Callander, Aberfoyle & Lochearnhead, Balquhidder & Strathyre*

After the walk: Pub/hotel in Aberfoyle

Walk outline

Loch Ard will be familiar to anyone driving along its northern shore via the narrow B829 that links Aberfoyle with Kinlochard. However by utilising the tracks that strike through Loch Ard Forest, then its beauty comes to the fore. The first half of the route passes stunning Lochan a' Ghleannain before dropping down to Loch Ard. Straightforward walking then extends alongside the loch's attractive southern bank back to the start.

Loch Ard

Loch Ard sits at the northern edge of Loch Ard Forest, which extends west from Aberfoyle to the foothills of Loch Lomond. The forest has larch, Scots pine, birch and oak trees and the corresponding wildlife includes deer, red squirrel and woodpecker. Loch Ard is sheltered by the high ground that surrounds its borders and offers superb views of Ben Lomond's eastern slopes. As well as being the source of the River Forth, Loch Ard is home to two Iron-Age crannogs. These ancient man-made islands are found in lochs across Scotland and Ireland and were used as easily-defended dwellings and places of refuge.

Lochan a' Ghleannain

Pine marten

The Walk

1. To reach the **Forestry Commission Milton Car Park** follow the **B829** from Aberfoyle for just over 1-mile then turn left at **Milton** (signposted Loch Ard Forest). Continue for another ½ mile into **Loch Ard Forest** where the car park sits on the left.

The route is waymarked with red posts throughout. Walk down to the access road and go straight on, signposted for Inversnaid, onto a wide track. Follow this as it sweeps left and once around a **metal barrier** continue in a southwesterly direction through attractive and peaceful mixed woodland.

Carry on alongside the steep slopes of **Dalzell Wood**, and keep straight on past a track on the left to reach the gorgeous **Lochan a' Ghleannain**.

Beside the loch is a bench making it a great location for a break. The loch is home to a couple of islands and is surrounded on all sides by woodland. When here look out for red squirrels amongst the pine trees and buzzard, jay, goldcrest and even osprey in and around the forest canopy.

2. Once past Lochan a' Ghleannain, the track rises steadily but soon levels off — *there are fine views to the north of Meall Dubh's long ridge*. Upon reaching a fork keep right, descend to a junction and turn left from where a steady descent gains another junction.

© Crown copyright and/or database right. All rights reserved. Licence number 100047867

Walk 7 – **Loch Ard** ♦ 47

Wonderful woods: *The tranquil surrounds of Loch Ard Forest with Loch Ard beyond*

3. Go right and continue, with the track granting the first glimpse of Loch Ard through the trees. At the next junction go left. Shortly afterwards the track ends and here turn left onto a path, which heads down to **Loch Ard** and through perhaps the most attractive section of the walk.

Beyond the tall pine and oak trees the view across the loch looks west to summit of Ben Lomond. Migrating geese may be seen flying above the surface of the loch. Also out on Loch Ard is the remains of the 14th century **Duke Murdoch's Castle**, *which stands on the* **island of Dundochdil** *(the Inhospitable Island). The castle may have been a hunting lodge and is thought to have been built by Murdoch, the Duke of Albany, a relative of King James I of Scotland.*

4. Head east along the path, with one short sharp climb taking you high above the loch. Here a fence on the left separates the path from a **sheer drop** and below is a **cave**, *allegedly used as a*

Sunset show: *The last rays of the sun colour the hills around Loch Ard*

hiding place by Rob Roy. Descend steadily down to the loch shore and continue back to the main forest track.

5. Turn left here and continue east alongside **Loch Ard** with fine views of the wooded slopes of Dun Dubh above the north shore. In due course the track passes **The Narrows**.

This ribbon of water is bounded with birch trees and provides a final superb vista across Loch Ard to Ben Lomond. The view of Scotland's southernmost Munro is a much more dramatic one than that from Loch Lomond, with the deep recess of Coire a' Fuar prominent.

The Narrows then opens back out and Loch Ard continues with a fine vista towards the steep slopes of Craigmore. Once around a **metal barrier**, keep straight on, keeping an eye out for colourful **boathouses** along the loch's edge.

At the head of Loch Ard pass round a final **barrier** and go past the beautifully located cottage of **Lochend** — to the left Loch Ard empties into the **River Forth**, which begins its journey to the Firth of Forth.

Walk 7 – **Loch Ard** ♦ 49

Keep on along a rough road and through a gate to reach a T-junction.

6. Here make a right turn onto the **Forestry Commission Milton access road** and follow this for 350 metres back to the car park, to complete the walk. ♦

Capercaillie

Even though they can grow to nearly 90 centimetres/ two feet in height, the capercaillie is an elusive bird. The best time to see them (although you are more likely to hear their distinctive clicking sound) is beneath the forest canopy at dawn, during spring, when the males display, or 'lek', to attract females. The numbers of capercaillie have seen a small resurgence in recent years due to habitat conservation within the National Park.

Loch Katrine in high summer

walk 8

Loch Katrine & Loch Arklet

Two lochs, a fabulous viewpoint and some intriguing history feature on this superb route

What to expect:
Private road, rough then firm path then minor road. One steady ascent

Distance/time: 8 kilometres/5 miles. Allow 2½ hours

Start: Car park at Stronachlachar Pier. Free but can get busy, particularly in summer. Stronachlachar is 11½ miles northwest of Aberfoyle

Grid ref: NN 404 102

Ordnance Survey Map: Explorer OL 39 Loch Lomond North *Tyndrum, Crianlarich & Arrochar*

After the walk: Café at Stronachlachar, hotel in Inversnaid, pubs in Aberfoyle

Walk outline

Loch Katrine and Loch Arklet have been the source of Glasgow's drinking water since 1914. They are separated by a wild expanse of moorland where air shafts trace the line of the remarkable underground aqueduct. A scenic stretch of road leads from Stronachlachar above Loch Katrine before a path rises across the moorland to gain the old Statute Labour Road. Beyond this a quiet road leads back to Stronachlachar.

Rob Roy

In 1817, seven years after writing his epic poem, *Lady of the Lake*, Sir Walter Scott published *Rob Roy*, a somewhat exaggerated account of Rob Roy MacGregor that romanticised his life. Rob Roy was born in 1671 at Glengyle, at the head of Loch Katrine, just a few miles from Stronachlachar. He was involved in the Jacobite uprising of 1688 and became a folk hero, chiefly because of his feud with James Graham, 1st Duke of Montrose. Rob Roy died at Balquhidder in 1734. Just like the *Lady of the Lake*, Scott's tale of Rob Roy brought many new visitors to The Trossachs.

Old 'Statute Labour Road'

Red grouse

The Walk

1. Begin from **Stronachlachar Pier**, home to an excellent café and where the SS Sir Walter Scott berths.

Follow the road west out of the car park. After 400-metres pass a gated track on the left then turn left onto a **private road**.

2. This runs southeast through woodland above Loch Katrine. After 500-metres the road crosses the **outlet of an aqueduct**.

The aqueduct flows from Loch Arklet to provide extra water for Loch Katrine, which had supplied Glasgow's water since 1859. The 34-mile Loch Katrine to Glasgow aqueduct remarkably uses no pumps, the water's flow wholly driven by gravity.

The road provides easy walking for a further 3 kilometres until it reaches a waymarked footpath on the right. However it's worth continuing for 100 metres to the striking **Royal Cottage**.

This was built as accommodation for Queen Victoria when opening the water scheme in 1859. However a local story tells how a 21-gun salute smashed all the windows — so she couldn't stay overnight.

3. Walk back to the woodland path on the left. At times muddy and a little overgrown, it rises steadily southwest, soon climbing above the trees to give a wonderful view across Loch Katrine.

Continue over moorland, passing a **ventilation shaft**, a legacy of the aqueduct's construction. Turn right at the next **shaft**, following a narrow path to the walk's **highest point**.

This spot has a wilder air and presents a superb view to Ben Lui's magnificent profile. To the southwest rises Ben Lomond.

4. Return to the main path and continue right of the next shaft. It then widens to a track, dropping down through a gate beneath **Tom Ard**. In due course a steeper descent culminates at a forestry track.

In the still of the evening: *Loch Arklet and the Arrochar Alps at sunset*

5. Turn right, walk northwest for 450 metres then take a path on the right, just before the B829.

6. A wonderful section of the walk continues across moorland following the old **Statute Labour Road** that once ran between Aberfoyle and Inversnaid.

Once through a gate, a breathtaking view of Loch Arklet and the Arrochar Alps fills the vista ahead with the path eventually gaining the **B829**.

7. Go right, follow the roadside verge for nearly 500 metres to a junction. Turn right and walk the final 750 metres back to the start to complete the walk. ♦

Old 'Military Road'

The paths and roads alongside Loch Arklet have been used for centuries. The old Military Road (which the B829 runs along today) was built around 300 years ago to serve the Inversnaid Garrison. English redcoats were stationed here to guard the road and control local rebels and cattle thieves, who, however, probably had a far better knowledge of the local topography.

54 ♦ TOP 10 WALKS

The Arrochar Alps reflected in Loch Lomond from Inversnaid

walk 9

Inversnaid & Loch Lomond

Dramatic waterfalls, superb views and lots of wildlife are all seen on this absorbing walk

What to expect:
Clear paths line the route which includes some steep ascents and descents

Distance/time: 4.5 kilometres/2¾ miles. Allow 1½ hours

Start: Rob Roy View car park. South side of the Inversnaid/Aberfoyle road, across a bridge over Arklet Water, 1 kilometre east of Inversnaid

Grid ref: NN 345 089

Ordnance Survey Map: Explorer OL 39 Loch Lomond North *Tyndrum, Crianlarich & Arrochar*

After the walk: Hotel at Inversnaid

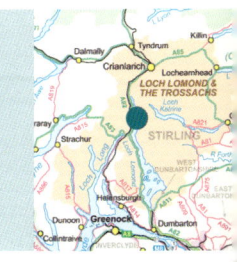

Walk outline

From high above Loch Lomond and Inversnaid a path, which at times can be boggy, drops down past the ruins of Clach Bhuidhe to reach Inversnaid and its spectacular waterfalls. A track then heads alongside Loch Lomond and through a nature reserve. A steep path through fine woodland provides more exquisite views before a return to Inversnaid. A section of The Great Trossachs Path climbs back to the start.

Inversnaid

Inversnaid translates beautifully from Gaelic as 'the mouth of the needle stream', describing the Snaid Burn that drops from the slopes of Beinn a Choin into Arklet Water — which itself flows into Loch Lomond at Inversnaid. The river cascades down a couple of striking waterfalls, and Gerard Manley Hopkins lauded the wild nature of the setting in his poem *Inversnaid*, written in 1881. Like the bulk of Loch Lomond's shores, Inversnaid is cloaked in beautiful, wildlife-rich oak woodland, part of which forms the Inversnaid RSPB Nature Reserve.

Inversnaid waterfalls

Feral black goat

The Walk

1. From the car park's western edge take the waymarked '**Great Trossachs Path**' through a gate. Almost immediately the path splits, so keep left (leaving the Great Trossachs Path) and walk through **Craigrostan Woods**. The route can be boggy as it drops gradually to pass through a gate onto open hillside.

The path descends through undergrowth where the views extend across Loch Lomond to the Arrochar Alps.

2. Beyond the **ruins of Clach Buidhe** descend steeply into oak woodland. Once through another gate the path approaches Inversnaid with the rumbling waterfalls now audible.

Pass a 'Great Trossachs Path' waymark on the right (this is for the return journey), bear right onto the '**West Highland Way**' and cross **two bridges** over the impressive **Arklet Water**. Steps then descend to the **Inversnaid Hotel**.

3. Walk around the front of the hotel to pick up the West Highland Way at the left corner of the **hotel car park**. Follow a track north along the loch shore into the **Inversnaid RSPB Nature Reserve**.

The track narrows to a path to reach a beach beside an old **boathouse**.

4. Bear right around the back of the boathouse then after 40-metres, just before a **bridge** over a burn, take the waymarked **RSPB Nature Trail** and climb through lovely oak woodland.

Steps make the going a little easier but it's a steep pull, leading high above Loch Lomond. As the route crosses a **bridge** the incline eases and continues to

© Crown copyright and/or database right. All rights reserved. Licence number 100047867

Loch shore: *Loch Lomond at Inversnaid*

a bench and a marvellous **viewpoint**. The path then drops steadily back to the West Highland Way.

5. Turn left, continue above the loch to the **boathouse** then retrace your steps back to the **Inversnaid Hotel**. Recross both bridges, bear left at a fork then turn left onto **The Great Trossachs Path**.

6. A stiff pull rises east above the **Arklet Water**, passing another spectacular **waterfall**. Above the treeline the gradient relents. It is then a simple, scenic stroll through a mixture of open hillside and woodland, passing through two more gates. At a junction bear left back onto the outward path and the final few metres to the car park to complete the walk. ♦

From farm to factory

A small farming community existed at Clach Buidhe until the late 18th century; the remains and outlines of cottages and farm enclosures can still be seen today. However, with the arrival of the Industrial Revolution the villagers eventually moved to Balfron, Fintry and the Vale of Leven lured by the promise of better housing and jobs in the increasingly busy textile industry.

Oaks and bluebells in the Great Trossachs Forest

walk 10

Loch Venachar

A complete circuit of gorgeous Loch Venachar makes for a long, energising and fantastically scenic route

What to expect:
Firm paths and tracks and minor roads. One steep ascent

Distance/time: 19.25 kilometres/12 miles. Allow 5 hours

Start: Glen Finglas Visitor Gateway (Lendrick Hill) Car Park. On the north side of the A821, 1.25 kilometres east of Brig o' Turk

Grid ref: NN 630 078

Ordnance Survey Map: Explorer OL 46 The Trossachs, *Callander, Aberfoyle & Lochearnhead, Balquhidder & Strathyre*

After the walk: Pub/tearoom in Brig o' Turk

Walk outline

A wonderful section of The Great Trossachs Path climbs above and along the northern shore of Loch Venachar, granting magnificent views of The Great Trossachs Forest. The route's inward half follows quiet roads that hug Loch Venachar's scenic southern bank to Invertrossachs after which a delightful path then forest track lead to Brig o' Turk's quiet surrounds. Once through the village it is an easy walk back to the start.

The Great Trossachs Forest

The Great Trossachs Forest covers an area of 160 square kilometres within the Loch Lomond and The Trossachs National Park. It's a landscape of huge environmental importance, containing areas of herb-rich alpine and sub-alpine grassland, ancient oak woodland, native Caledonian pinewoods, woodland pasture, moorland and montane scrub — all supporting a vast diversity of flora and fauna, much of it rare and protected. Since 2009 an incredible 1.5 million native trees, such as birch, rowan, juniper, hazel and alder have been planted. Striking through the heart of the forest is The Great Trossachs Path, a superb 30-mile trail linking Callander and Inversnaid.

The Great Trossachs Path

Black-throated diver

Horn of plenty: *Loch Venachar means 'horn-shaped loch'*

The Walk

1. Glen Finglas Visitor Gateway has an excellent **interpretation centre**. From here take the **bridge** over a burn onto the waymarked **Great Trossachs Path**. Beyond a gate, bear left and rise steadily through ash and oak woodland, the path soon swinging right to pass a **ruined farmstead**.

This was once part of the Drippen township which was abandoned during the mid 19th century. A bench is a good excuse to take in the rugged peak of Ben Venue and the long finger of Loch Venachar.

2. In due course the path forks so keep right and continue a gradual ascent east, beneath the slopes of **Stuc Odhar** with the view now extending to Loch Achray and Loch Drunkie.

Walk 10 – **Loch Venachar** ♦ 61

The path undulates easily across **moorland**, *granting the chance to spot deer, pearl-bordered fritillary butterfly and golden eagle.*

Beyond the woodland of **Dubh Cnoc**, where views of Callander and Stuc a Chroin open out, the path drops down to a track. Turn left and descend to the gorgeous **Milton Glen Burn**, *a favourite spot for dipper.*

3. A **footbridge** spans the burn, after which keep straight on through a gate to a T-junction. Keep right then left when the path forks and continue beneath the lower slopes of **Ben Ledi**.

After going straight on at a crossroads, above the **ruin of Coilantogle**, continue for another 1km to a junction (just before this a path peels left and rises onto the summit of Dun Mor).

4. Turn right for Invertrossachs (left provides a short detour to **Sampson's Putting Stone**, a glacial erratic left behind after the last Ice Age), leaving The Great Trossachs Path for now, and drop down through a gate.

Carefully cross the **A821** onto a minor road and follow this over the old packhorse **Gartchonzie Bridge** that spans the **Eas Gobhain**.

At its far end turn right for Invertrossachs (also part of the National Cycling Network route 7) and follow a quiet, narrow road southwest (watch out for traffic) as it travels alongside **Loch Venachar**, *which is thought to mean 'horn-shaped loch'.*

A couple of picnic spots are ideal for a break and to enjoy wildlife that includes geese and black-throated diver as well as superb views of Ben Ledi and Ben Venue.

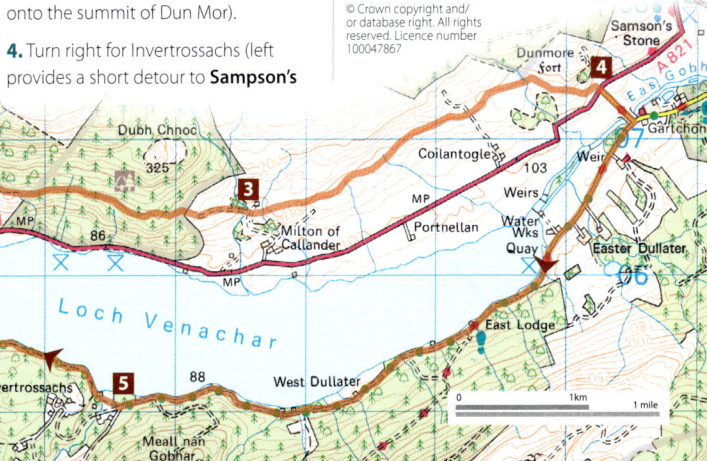

© Crown copyright and/or database right. All rights reserved. Licence number 100047867

Mellow yellow: *Banks of gorse brighten the view over Loch Venachar from Milton Fort*

After 2 kilometres the road passes **East Lodge** and enters **Invertrossachs Estate** where the road passes **Loch Venachar Sailing Club**. It then continues easily, with little navigational issues, allowing the scenery and wildlife to come to the fore.

5. Just before reaching the tiny settlement of **Invertrossachs** turn right through a gate (signposted NCN 7), and follow a path into woodland, then alongside the loch — it is one of the finest sections of the route.

Loch Venachar is eventually left behind as the path continues beside the broad river system of the **Black Water**, culminating at **Forest Drive**. Bear right onto this wide track (used by traffic during the summer months), *granting lovely views of Ben A'an and Ben Vane*.

After it swings right over a **stone bridge** the track passes through a gate beside a cattle grid then drops down to **The Great Trossachs Path** at a junction beside **Achray Farm**.

6. Turn right, go through a gate and walk through this working farm. After the track sweeps left over an old **stone**

Walk 10 – **Loch Venachar** ♦ 63

bridge spanning the **Black Water** continue to the **A821** at **Brig o' Turk**. Go right and follow the pavement through this quiet little village, which translates from Gaelic as 'Bridge of the Pig'.

Beyond Brig o' Turk a path runs parallel with the road. At its end go through a gate, carefully cross the A821, pass through another gate then bear right and follow a path back to **Lendrick Hill** to complete the walk. ♦

'Big fort'
Dunmore rises near Loch Venachar's northeastern shore and, in Gaelic, means 'the Large Fort'. Archaeologists suggest a thriving community and their livestock lived here some 2,000 years ago. The fort contains a number of terraced walls, the size and extent of which suggest that a tribal leader of great importance lived within the settlement. Remember, walls were built not just for security; they were a symbol of power and status too.

Useful Information

Loch Lomond and The Trossachs Tourism
Visit Scotland's official website covers everything from accommodation and events to attractions and adventure. **www.visitscotland.com/destinations-maps/loch-lomond-trossachs-forth-valley/**

Loch Lomond and The Trossachs National Park
The Loch Lomond and the Trossachs National Park website also has information on things to see and do, plus maps, webcams and news. **www.lochlomond-trossachs.org/**

Tourist Information Centres
The main TICs provide free information on everything from accommodation and travel to what's on and walking advice.

Aberfoyle	01877 382 221	info@visitscotland.com
Balloch	01389 753 533	info@visitscotland.com
Balmaha	01389 722 100	info@lochlomond-trossachs.org
Callander	01877 330 342	info@visitscotland.com
Luss	01436 860 229	purdiesofluss@hotmail.co.uk

Steamers and Ferries
Loch Lomond

Balloch & Luss	01389 752 376	www.sweeneyscruiseco.com info@sweeneyscruiseco.com
Luss & Balmaha	01389 752 376	www.sweeneyscruiseco.com info@sweeneyscruiseco.com
Rowardennan & Luss	01301 702 356	www.cruiselochlomond.co.uk stuart@cruiselochlomond.co.uk
Tarbet & Inversnaid	01301 702 356	www.cruiselochlomond.co.uk stuart@cruiselochlomond.co.uk
Loch Katrine	01877 376315/6	www.lochkatrine.com enquiries@lochkatrine.com

Weather
Three day weather forecast for Loch Lomond and The Trossachs National Park:
www.mwis.org.uk/scottish-forecast/WH/
www.mwis.org.uk/scottish-forecast/SH/